Only If They Knew

"Echoes of the Heart:
A Collection of Melancholic Verses"

Tejaswani Bakshi

BlueRose ONE .com
Stories Matter
NewDelhi • London

BLUEROSE PUBLISHERS
India | U.K.

For permissions requests or inquiries regarding this publication, please contact:

BLUEROSE PUBLISHERS
www.BlueRoseONE.com
info@bluerosepublishers.com
+91 8882 898 898
+4407342408967

ISBN: 978-93-6261-470-4

Cover design: Tahira
Typesetting: Tanya Raj Upadhyay

First Edition: May 2024

To everyone,

who felt excluded by the world but found home in poetry.

Table of Contents

Playlist

Happy – NF
Love In The Dark – Adele
Champagne Problems – Taylor Swift
If You Want Love – NF
Bruises – Lewis Capaldi
Heads In The Clouds – Hayd
Outsider – Rachel Grae
Easy On Me – Adele
Two Ghosts – Harry styles
Heal – Tom Odell
Please Notice – Christian Leave
Cigarette – Shaya Zamora
Jealousy, Jealousy – Olivia Rodrigo
Family Line – Conan Gray
Another Love – Tom Odell
Demons – Imagine Dragons
You're Losing Me – Taylor Swift
Look At The Time – Sawyer Hill
Let You Down – NF
Girl Crush – Little Big Town
Falling – Harry Styles
Daylight – David Kushner
Ghost Town – Benson Boone
Favorite Crime – Olivia Rodrigo

Matilda – Harry Styles

Angels Like You – Miley Cyrus

Exile – Taylor Swift (feat. Bon Iver)

Hate Myself – NF

Love You Goodbye – One direction

Changes – Hyad

Midnight Rain – Taylor Swift

Paralyzed – NF

This Town – Niall Horan

July – Noah Cyrus

New Friends – Jordana Bryant

Where's My Love – SYML

Human – Rag'n'Bone Man

I Guess I'm In Love – Clinton Kane

My Tears Ricochet – Taylor Swift

Do you ever just look at yourself in the mirror and think that maybe being a kid was better than what you've become now?

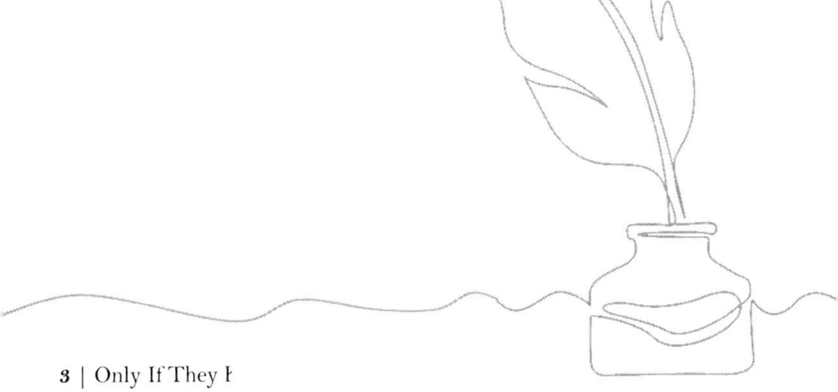

'Not Six Anymore'

I remember the dress
My little pink dress
It had a bow in the back
Pick flowers and white pearls on the top.

The white ballet sandals
They were worn-out
But I still wouldn't let them go
Oh! My white little sandals that I wore.

That dress and those shoes
Made me feel beautiful
More than any makeup would ever do
Back when pink was my favourite colour
Back when I believed that fairy tales were real.

When I played and danced
Screamed and cried
But also laughed and smiled
Back when I was a child.

But I'm not six anymore
Now I have a closet that's filled with black

Bows, pearls and flowers
No, I cannot wear them anymore.

Now, I only wear the plain shoes that I own
Because in sandals I'm too girly
And heels make me too tall for a girl.
My shoes, they are worn-out still
But not in the same way they used to be.

Now I wear makeup even to hide that one little freckle
Hoping one day,
Maybe someday I'll feel beautiful again.

I've grown to hate pink
Because it makes me feel too weak
I keep my hair short at all times
Because long hair is too feminine.

I got to know that fairy tales,
They don't exist
The only thing that still remains
Are the nightmares that I relive.

All the playfulness and the dances are long forgotten
I still scream and cry
But I rarely laugh and smile.
I hate what growing up has made me like.

The kid I once knew is now gone
All I can do is miss that little girl I once was
Because now, I am not six anymore.

Is it weird to like things that have been ruined?

'The Broken Things'

I love broken things
And hate everything that's proper and fixed
Because it reminds me of something I can never be.
Broken feels homely
Whereas wholeness it scares me.

Destruction,
It always comes easier
Give me a glass,
And I'll break it
Just to feel myself bleed.
Pain is a familiar feeling
But not being hurt is a strange story.

I did try to fix everything once
Back when I was a kid
I saw my mom fix everything
I thought that is how it has to be
When something breaks
You put it back the same.

But that was all before,
Back when I didn't know that broken things can never be whole.

A broken house
It can never be complete.
A broken soul
It can never be healed.

No matter,
How hard you try to put back a broken mirror
The cracks,
They never leave.

But beauty,
It lies in the eyes of the beholder.

Being complete might be perfect
But oh,
Being torn apart is chaotic.
And me,
I'm a lover of chaos
I'd rather be chaotic and distributed
And not perfect at all.

So yes,
I love broken things
And I'd rather spend all eternity loving every single, shattering and lonely piece
And never try to fix and heal.

Because you see,
A broken house
It can never be complete,
So, it becomes the home to many stories.

And,

A broken soul
It can never be healed,
So, it becomes the poet behind every poetry.

Hopeless romantic? Yup, that's me.

'A Soul For A Soul'

I want that lust for soul kind of love
I want you to crave for me
I want you to break only for me
Starving for my touch.

I want all of your tears
Your rage and your sadness even
I don't just want the happy things
The movie nights or the fancy getaway rides
I want to see the places you been hurt
Scars that you've been hiding from the world.

Tell me how others ripped you apart
Tell me all your needs and wants
Tell me when was the last time you cried
And tell me how you're losing the high of life.

All the sad things
Things that nobody else would want to hear
Say them out aloud to me
Let me cry my tears
Let me hold you while you escape
Let me have your soul and I'll give you mine in exchange.

Never thought I would ever believe that 'Hurt people always hurt people'

But then life happened.

'The Ocean'

When I met you
I was drowning
"And now". You ask?
Now I am 'the ocean'.
Reason behind so many lost souls
The mystery
Nobody wants to solve.

You were 'the ocean' before me
As selfish as one could be
You floated me to the shore
Just so you could pass me the curse.

And now that I am 'the ocean'
No matter,
How hard I try
To not let people die
I fail every time.

I am the tsunami
Drowning all my friends
I am the cause
With no end.
So, I'll pass on this curse to somebody else.

Do you think that letting go is the hardest?

'Let You Go'

How do I let you go?
After all these months
How can I sleep knowing
I won't wake up to your call?
Yes, yes I told you it was over
But I didn't want you gone just yet.

I told you "I'm lost"
Hoping you'll be the map
Out of this maze
But you only stood there
As my hardest obstacle.

I can pretend that I moved on
Pretend to be happy
That your life is taking on
But it kills me to see you smile
Now that I am not the reason why.

I am selfish
If that what it is
But I hate seeing you wear the shirt

That I gifted.

So,
How do I let you go?
How can I not be the one you hold close?

Love is not always rainbow and sunshine. Now, is it?
Sometimes, it is dark but I guess that's the best kind.

'Him And I'

I'm a poet
With no words to write
Maybe I've been cursed
Cursed by his intoxicating sight.

Not my prince charming
He's my dark knight.
He said "I'm incapable of anything good"
Told him "So am I".

If I'm a wave
He is my ocean
And if he's the moon
I'll be his sky.

Our love is like fire
Hot and always burning
The flames consume everything around
Except him and I.

He's like heaven in hell
The place I dwell
The home that I crave.

His eyes are made to destroy
His smile is meant to ruin.

I'm his prayer
And he's my religion.
If I'm an addict
Then he is my drug.
If he's a sin
Then I'm the biggest sinner.

His touch is warm
With a heart that's wrecked
He's the chaos
Who thrives on darkness.
He's like poison meant to break and kill
Yet somehow all I need is him.

He's my destiny
My obsession
My faith
My undoing
My saviour
My passion
My everything.

"I don't care what others think about me."
the biggest lie I ever said.

'Strangers'

I love strangers
Strangers who will never become friends with me
Random people who smile at me while in the elevator
Stranger for whom I'll hold the door in the grocery store.
I am socially awkward all the time
But only when I am out with my friends
Because I feel like they see too much
And then the next thing I know is how insecure I have always been.
Whenever I am out with them
I realize how it is better to rot in my bed instead.
My snorting laugh that I hide
How I don't want them to see
The crinkles by my eyes when I smile
Or how I bite my lip every time I try to speak
Because nobody is ever listening to me.
That is why I always like strangers better
They'll not see how my stomach folds when I sit
Or how I get all sweaty whenever in unknown spaces
They'll only see my kindness
And how I smiled back at them in the elevator.

I am the villain in somebody's story too.
That is fine,
I guess.

'The Dying Tale'

It hurts me to see you like this
Swelled eyes and that shiver in your voice
It hurts me to break your heart
Telling you that we were never meant to last.

The roses you gave me that day
They died on the same bench
With the love that we once shared
I left you all alone
Maybe I had to break your heart just because you've never been hurt.

It's not like I never loved you
I did with everything I had
But that is not enough for me to stay
And your ignorance has pushed me away.

I want you to know
That it hurts me too
And I hate myself for what I did to you
I did give you warning signs
Maybe I should've been more honest
Maybe I should've told you
I am tired of never being the one receiving your smiles.

I wanted the hurt
And you wanted the love
The love I don't have to offer
I am sorry that I made you cry
And I am sorry that I was the one who said goodbye.

Yeah, I know breakups hurt but not as much as seeing the person you trusted the most leave you at your worst.

'Somebody That I used To Know'

We've changed
You and I
We no longer love the things
That we once liked.

You look different
I see that you've changed your style
Tell me,
Do you still like Backstreet Boys?
And does watching Titanic still make you cry?

You've grown your hair out
Just like the memories
That you have outgrown now.
Do you still visit the places that we once went to?
Or do you avoid them as much as I do?

You have new friends now
People I know nothing about
The worst heartbreak I've ever felt
The day when you said
That I am a horrible friend.

Weren't we supposed to be the friends
Who sticks together till the very end?
Now look at us,
We are strangers again
But with memories shared.

You already replaced me
'The new best friend'
She knows you all too well
Just like I did once
When we were best of friends.

"Learn to take a joke."

No, maybe you should learn how to shut your mouth.

'The Worst Kind Of Scars'

Sticks and stones may break my bones,
But words can tear my heart apart.
Like a broken mirror,
Shattered all across the room.
The speech that in-fact was a joke,
Could be the ghost of all.
Like the time marks shall pass
It is the words that'll last.

"How are you?"
The answer to this is always "I'm fine."
Because why would anyone want to know about how I actually am?

'Raw, Scared, Broken And Weak'

"I'm fine", I say
With the smile
That I fake
While being trapped in a cage.
Tied with threads
That are turning into chains.

My laughter that is forgotten
And the voice that is quite
Made friends with the darkness
And drowning in my own created silence.

"I'm fine", I tell them
Just to make believe
That one day
There will be truth in the words I speak.

Maybe one day
They'll see the tears behind the veil.
They'll know the lie
I hide behind.

When,
I hold the gun with my own hands.
And when I pull the trigger
While I choke on my blood and tears
Then, they'll see me for me
They'll know who I truly am
Raw, scared, broken and weak.

I wish I was a doll
Because that way I wouldn't be real.

'Only A Doll'

It's the way I sit
The way I stand
The way I walk
The way I talk.
Too fat or too thin
Too tall or too short.
What do I wear?
What is the length of my hair?
Am I too loud?
Maybe not polite enough.

I am a doll
Plastic with only skin
And no feelings at all.

I can have an opinion
Only if it's the same as yours
I can stand my own ground
Until it's you I'm talking about
I have to smile
Remember to always be kind
Even if I'm dying inside.

Because all I am is a doll
Plastic with only skin
And no feelings at all.

Maybe a sinner can never be condoned

'Can A Sinner Be Forgiven?'

I can be a lover
But never in a romanticizing way
I can't show you care
All I have are stained nights to offer.

I want to save you
But how can I?
When I'm a burning house
And everything
Everything close to me is already destined to die.

But oh!
Touching you felt magical
Like somehow, I've cheated my way into heaven
Like maybe all my sins were condoned
Even thought that having you close
Is my only home.

Being with you
It was like a dream
Meant to end
The way it did.

I watched you go
Still couldn't blame you though
Because how could you survive a sinking ship?
How could you love me
After everything that I've done?
How could you stay
After I pushed you away?

Will my sins ever be forgiven
Or will I continue existing as a shell more than a human?

Is it better to be 'the silent kid' or 'the popular kid'?

'The Main Lead'

You and me
We are so different
You are the friend
Everyone likes
The main character of every party night
Never alone
Always with a friend to stand by.

And me,
I am just another lost soul
Living in the shadows of all
While you made a life out of lies
I made mine through sacrifice.

I stay behind
And watch you fit in just right.
I've seen your Instagram stories
All the laughter and smiles
The giggles and the inside jokes you hide.

Oh! You are so cool
Everyone wants to be like you.
On top of the world
But your world isn't even real.

So don't tell me
That you know how I feel.
I am just another shy, silent kid
And you,
You are the main lead.

Wouldn't it be awesome if forgiving and forgetting was as simple and easy as snapping your fingers together?

'Forgive And Forget'

They say "Forgive and forget"
How can I forget him
Those brown eyes
Those little smiles
He was the colour in my frame
The bane of my existence
Like that feeling of apricity
In the winter season.

He was like the weekend
After a long week
The rainbow
In the rainy streak
Like that one light
On the dark street
His eyes shone more than any jewel
He was an angel.

So, no I cannot forget him
No matter what I do
He's tamed on my skin and bones
A scar on my heart and soul.

I cannot forgive him either
For all the times
I cried myself to sleep
When I gasped and gasped
For every single breath I need.

The times
When I hated myself
To the times
When I wanted me dead.
Every moment that I spent changing myself
Thinking he'd want me if I was different.

He stabbed my back
Pierced through my heart
Restraint my neck
While I choked on my own thoughts.
Oh! My angel did it all.

I cannot be his lover anymore
I cannot be his friend either.
So, I'll settle for the memories
While trying to escape everything that happened.

True love is always raw and chaotic.

'Love You'

Be my grace
And I will happily follow you to my grave.
If you are hate
I will still worship you the same.

Doesn't matter if you are night
I will be your moon light.
I will become a shield
If it's the storms that make you feel weak.

If you fall
I will hold you
While we fall together.
If you are a belladonna
I will still name you my favourite flower.

I don't only want to be yours
Till the death do us apart
But even after and beyond.

And only if you are the death
I will accept every bit of you with the rest.

Do the 'What if's' haunt you too or is it just me?

'The What If's'

I feel like I'm drowning
But when I reach the end
I know that I will resurface as always
I'll come back up gasping
Cleaning the air
While somehow breathing in the smoke
To feel the distance between death and me
Come to halt but still not disappear.

To see with my bare eyes
The life leaving my body
Just never completely
The sense of losing control
Just to regain it all over again.

What if the next time I never come back?
Will it be the end of all
Maybe the start of a new war
Will I struggle to drag in enough air?

Will I resist the urge once for all?
Or I'll give in to what waits for me?
Simply just letting every bit slip.

But would it change everything or nothing at all?
Would it be a sign of my loss
Or the scream of my win?
Perhaps it won't be anything at all.

What is the meaning of life if not love?

'Someone'

I want to hate love
But I stop every time
Before crossing that line.

I believe that somewhere there is someone just like me
Someone who loves the same as I do
We see the world with the same eyes
"I saw this and thought of you"
Type of love
"I know you are sleeping but"
Kind of texts
Waking up to the 'good morning' notifications
And 'I love you' every night before bed.

Two bodies
But one soul
Two people with different homes
But only one place where they truly belong.

Someone who sends me the picture of how pretty the sky looks
And someone who knows why grey is my favourite colour
Someone who knows how I like my coffee in the morning
And how I only like hot chocolate with marshmallows in it.

Someone who knows why I hate loud noises
And why I find nights comforting
Someone who will never let me sleep with teary eyes
And someone who will hear my silence.

Someone who will ask what my current read was about
And someone who loves the rain the way that I do
Someone who will fight for me to stay
Who will make me feel 'enough' every day.

Someone just like me,
A hopeless romantic, as they say
Who reads those silly romantic novels
And believes that they'll find someone just like the books.

Someone just like me,
Our hearts are bruised
Broken one to many times
But that spark of love never dims
And that flicker of hope to find someone to love
It always stays the same.

Is it just me or the 'situationships'
confuse you all too?

'What Are We?'

Look into my eyes
Tell me what you find
Do you see the thoughts I hide
And the questions I keep inside?

Tell me
What are we?
Are we a sinking ship
Or are we floating above the sea?

Will I get your love and smiles
Or only lust and lies
Are you the one I let in
Or the one whom I shouldn't keep?

Do I wake up in your arms
Or do I have to sneak out before your alarm goes off
Will I get to see new days with you
Or will yours be the number I couldn't reach to?

Tell me,
If you think that we are meant to be
Or are we just two lost souls
Trying to be less lonely?

Do I get to call you my home
Or will yours be the heart
I could never own.
Will you hold my hand
Or will you leave me behind?
Will the I love you' s ever mean a thing
Or will we just pretend
Till the day we finally stop lying?

So, tell me
Will our love write history
Or will we be the unsolved mystery
Will ours be a happy ending
Or just another incomplete story?

Why can't we treat each other as just humans?

'Just Human'

Why can't they let me be just a person?
Nothing more
Nothing less
Just a human.

Why does the colour of my skin
Defines me less of a person
When our heart beats the same.

Do the tattoos on my body
Says that I am insincere and impulsive?
When it's actually quite the opposite.

Why does what I wear
Makes them the judge of my character?
When it's nothing more than just a fabric draped to hide my insecure presence.

I need to be a certain way
Or else I am not acceptable
In the society they've made
Why is it a sin
to be comfortable in my own skin?

And if I don't want to settle down
Does it mean that I am immature?
But why can't my way of living be different than what they chose?

Do they know that the blood in our veins
Runs and bleeds the same
Do they know that my skin and bones hurt too
Just like theirs do
My eyes they do shed tears
We all break the same beneath the layers.

Why can't they let me be just a person?
Nothing more
Nothing less
Just a human.

I always thought growing up is what makes everything better.

Well, news flash-

It doesn't.

'A Silent Loner'

When I was a child
I always wanted to grow up quick
But now that I am older
I miss something I never was
A kid.

Instead of staying inside a burning house
I should've gone outside to live somehow
Instead of crying silent under the sheets
I should've been playing in the crowded streets.

As a child
I wondered what my future was like
Will I be able to make friends
Or will it always be hard for me to fit in
Now I have found home in my loneliness
Comfort in my own created silence.

People tell me
That I am mature for my age

This compliment that I hate
Because all I want is to be a kid again.

Then this time I'll do it all right
And maybe then I'll not be jealous
When someone tells me
How a happy childhood feels like.

I thought growing up would make all the undeniable hurt stop
But little did I know
This confusion it never ends
And every night I still ask myself
"What did I do to deserve any of this?"

Have you ever fallen out of love?

'The Opposite Of Love'

I don't think that the opposite of love is hate
Because how can it be?
I think the opposite of love is losing interest.

Losing interest in explaining yourself
Losing interest in making things work
Losing interest in telling them how your day was
Losing interest in pretending to be someone you are not
Losing interest in being gaslighted and manipulated
Losing interest in putting them first
Losing interest in the bare minimum they give
Losing interest in their lies and the stupid games they play
Losing interest in staying the same.

More than that
I feel the opposite of love has always been losing but never hate.
Losing interest
Losing hope
Losing yourself
While trying to be someone they love.

Do you ever think about the questions to which nobody knows the answers?

'Once You Die'

I often wonder what happens once you die
Is it the same as living a life?
Does the world become all black and white
Or do you find peace after closing your eyes for that one last time?

Am I suppose to make amends in my afterlife?
But that is all I do in this life
Do I reminisce about everything I did?
That's all I do still
Think about the past
And blind myself to the future because I am too scared to open my eyes.

I know, I know death is the only truth
And I shall face it too
But what does death look like?
Maybe it is a friend
A friend who stays constant through all.
But then why are people scared to die?
Do they not want their book to end?

Maybe people are just scared
Scared to leave their story incomplete

Still, why does it matter?
Because once you are gone, you are gone for good, I guess.

So, do I wait for death?
Or do I just live my life
And then when I am eighty, I should start calling for death to take me.

Death is like a half truth
The other part is not the lie but something only the dead would know
Maybe death is nothing but a loophole.
But then again, what happens once you die?

I never want to be a disappointment but even more than that I never want to be the one who is disappointed.

'Let You Down'

I never wanted to let you down
And I am sorry
For stepping out now.

I smiled
Happy, with only scrappy bits of affection you provide
Always learned
That beggars can't be choosers
So, I survived while dying on the inside.

You've taught me everything that I know
Humans are the worst type of monsters
The biggest lesson of all.

You've made me familiar with hate
But then how am I addicted to the love
That you never gave?

How do I blame you
When you've been hurt too?
But I cannot protect you no more
My blood is running cold
And my heart is growing a hole.

I wish
I could stay
But if I do
I cannot heal the wounds that you gave
Because, you keep on tearing my stitches apart
And then you start playing the victim card.

You break my heart
When you treat me like a puppet doll
Say the lies that you've mastered
And then you laugh the evil laughter.

I never wanted to let you down
But I want to live
And not die trying to breathe somehow
It is either you or me
I am sorry,
For I am not what you wanted me to be.

Now,
It is my time to leave.

Have you ever been in a situation where nothing really makes sense?

'Come Home'

I will wait by the door
Hoping you will come home.
I search for you in every crowded room
Thinking,
Maybe you are searching for me too.

Without you everything has stopped making sense
Straight lines,
They turned into circles
The roof of my house
Turned into a cave
I live under.

I pick the petals
Will you return or will you not
Will I sleep in this bed on my own
Or will you not let me be alone?

Look at this,
The pathetic mess that you've made me
I am in pain
And you are my only relief.

How could you not return

To the things we made from love
How could you stay away for long
When you promised that you'll stay with me
No matter what.

I guess promises as just words
Words that you can no longer remember
But how could you leave behind
The home we built together?

I want you,
I need you,
So, I will stay by the door
Waiting for you to come home.

Do you think that love is meant to hurt?

'A Game Of Love And Hate'

They say "keep your friends close
But your enemies closer"
So, what are you?
Are you my friend, my enemy or my lover?

Never mind,
I will keep you close anyway
Maybe secretly,
I do love this game of Love and Hate.

You are like razor to my skin
Salt to my wounds
The reason behind every tear that I cry
Then why do I never let you go?
And why do I still keep you close?

Maybe,
I am a masochist
Living through the pain that you give

But you my love,
You are even worse
Because you love watching me suffer.

Afterall, it is just a game
Isn't it?
A game of love and hate.

I always want to be the poet and never the poem.

'The Next Poem'

They say "being loved by a writer is a blessing"
Well, is it a blessing or a curse?
I can make you immortal
Write about your beautiful existence on my paper
Until one day when everything changes
What we thought was the garden of flowers
It was all roses with thorns.
I'll write about you still
Could've would've should've feelings
You'll always stay immortal
But somebody will become a soul with no end too
When I'll write about them just like I wrote about you.

Do you ever hate someone without having a good reason to actually hate them?

'Hate To Hate Her'

I am a girl's girl
Then why do I hate her?
It kills me
Seeing her arm wrapped around your shoulder
Watch you give her the love
I begged for
Because if she never existed
Maybe then I would've saved this sinking love of ours.

She is everything
That I am not
I am impulsive
And she's patient
I am ruined
And she is a perfect angel.

I hate the glow on her face
The one when you show her off
Like she is a new trophy
The kind, one would cheat to win.
The blush on her face
Drives me crazy
And the wise thoughts she speak
Always been so above me.

The way you look at her
Like she is the most beautiful girl
Makes me hate her even more
And it is disgusting to see
How you give her everything
That I once asked for me.

She is so well put
Always the kind type
Her and I
We are like parallel lines
Maybe it was all in my head
And were you never really mine?

Have you ever had that love-hate relation with someone?

'Also My Father's Daughter'

I just want to be my mother's daughter
Just like her
Beautiful, polite
And always the loving kind.

But,
I also am my father's daughter
I've got his anger, ignorance
And just like him
I am also a poison.

Everyone tells me
I look so alike my mother
These words that I love to hear
Still,
How can I forget
The blood in my veins
It is the same as my father's.

I have his smile
Also, his eyes
The truth I hide my way
Like how he always lied with such ease
I am like him

More than I would ever admit.

My mom is the 'forgiving' kind
My dad was the 'never set you free' type
And I am both
Forgiving but never letting anything go
And,
This is the loneliest combination of all.

Why can't I just be like my mom?
Why can't I blame him for everything that is wrong?
Well, I guess that is the price you pay
For loving someone
Whom you should hate.

I only want to be my mother's daughter
But how can I?
When my last name is the same as my father's.

How can they love someone they can't tell is dying?

'Dripping Blood'

You ask me
"What have I ever done to you?"
Can't you see my crimson blood dripping down your hands
Your knife
It screams my name
And my back is filled with your stabs.

Tell me,
Tell me that I am overreacting still
Tell me that you are not killing me
And this all is just a really bad dream
But then can't you see that I am dying
And I can no longer breathe.

Tell me how much you love me
Just to break me again
Show me all the highs
Just to push me down that cliff
Because monsters like you don't live under any bed
They walk around with that same smile
In the broad daylight.

My bandages are full now
Full on my blood, tears and sweat

And I am so tired of being the bravest soldier
Trying to be your favourite
Hoping I will get the reward that I deserve
Reward that I have long waited for.

And then when we meet next
Ask me again,
"What have I ever done to you?"
I'll smile and say
"It was me and never you."
I will tell you that it was all my fault
Because I am the one who is always wrong
It was me,
Who was an undeserving mess
Always unworthy of you and your 'loving self'.

I have always been a fan of dark romance.
The maddening passion and the unhealthy obsession.

'The Eternal Kind Of Thing'

If you are the pain
Then I don't want any cure
If you are the night
Then I don't want to see the sun rise ever again
If you are the cliff
Then I'll fall and fall until there's nothing left of me
And if you are a battle
Then I will never let the fights end ever.

If you are the ashes
Then I'll burn my flesh to see you rise
If you are the poison smoke
Then I'll fill my lungs with you
If you are not the one for me
Then I'll fight the heavens above to make it happen
And if you are a dream
Then I'll sleep forever.

If you are a writer
Then I'll be your ink
If you are the stones
Then I'll walk bare feet until you imprint yourself on me
If you are the water
Then I'll drown and drown

And If you are the blade
Then I'll let you cut through my skin.

If you are a burning candle
Then I'll hold you with my naked hands
If you are the mountains
Then I'll be the flowing river
If you are the rain
Then I'll be your thunder
And If you are the death
Then I'll kill myself in every life just so we are always together.

I wonder, would it make any difference if the silent battles we fought were not so silent?

'Only If They Knew'

Only if they knew
That I am scared too
Will they reach for me
Or will they leave me be?

Only if they could see
The life,
So slowly leaving my body
And how quiet I have lately been.

Only if they knew
The harsh words they speak
Are the same ones
That my brain repeats.

Only if they could see
I am on my knees
The tears on my cheeks
Whispering the silent prayers for help
Waiting for someone to lift me
And put me back up on my feet.

Only if they knew
That I am a human too

I have made my mistakes
And paid for them with pain.

Only if they could see
The sleepless nights
Or the night where I cry myself to sleep
Maybe then they'd love
And care for me.

Only if they knew
That I am delicate too
I have been hurt
And I break as easily as everyone else do.

Only if they could see
That I was a kid
Forced to grow up very quick
Can't they see
That I am too weak
Then why can they not be easy on me?

Acknowledgements

The only person I want to thank is my mother. Without your love and support I am nothing. Thank you for supporting me all the way and believing in me. Mumma, you are the strongest and the kindest person I have ever known. I would've never been able to write a book if it wasn't for the encouragement you gave.

I could never thank you enough for all the things you've done for me and our family. You really are a superwoman. I love you so very much.

This book is for you and your trust in me. I hope I made you proud.

About the playlist in the start of the book- I love music (who doesn't). Those songs relate to the book in some way that I cannot explain. Music has always been there for me when humans weren't. I guess I just wanted to share that with you all too.

The playlist 'Only If They Knew' is available on Spotify.